SUNKEN SHIPS & TREASURE

Beautiful example of minted piece of eight found on the
H.M.S. Association, *lost off the Scilly Isles in 1707.*

SUNKEN SHIPS
& TREASURE

AN INTERNATIONAL
OCEANOGRAPHIC
FOUNDATION
SELECTION

ATHENEUM   NEW YORK   1986

written
& illustrated
with photographs
by JOHN
CHRISTOPHER
FINE

Atheneum
Macmillan Publishing Company
866 Third Avenue, New York, NY 10022

Type set by Fisher Composition, Inc., New York City
Printed & bound by the Toppan Printing Company, Inc., Hong Kong
Designed by Mary Ahern

First Edition
10 9 8 7 6 5 4 3 2 1

Library of Congress Cataloging in Publication Data

Fine, John Christopher.
  Sunken ships and treasure.

  Bibliography: p. 114.
  Includes index.
  1. Shipwrecks — Juvenile literature.   2. Treasure-
trove — Juvenile literature.   I. Title.
G525.F495   1986   910.4'53   86-3652
ISBN 0-689-31280-6

Title page: *This diver is using an underwater metal
detector to locate coins buried in the sand.*

Contents

SUNKEN SHIPS & TREASURE

Deep in the crews quarters of sunken Japanese warship in Truk Lagoon, divers discover skulls of sailors who lost their lives during the furious attack.

Molly is the only dolphin in the world trained to use her natural echolocation to find treasure. The high frequency signals Molly sends out act as radar underwater, enabling her to find coins, even those buried under silt and sand. Here Molly brings a coin back to her handler.

TO THE
HESITATING PURCHASER

If sailor tales to sailor tunes,
Storm and adventure, heat and cold,
If schooners, islands, and maroons,
And Buccaneers and buried Gold,
And all the old romance, retold,
Exactly in the ancient way,
Can please, as me they pleased of old,
The wiser youngsters of today:

So be it, and fall on! If not,
If studious youth no longer crave,
His ancient appetites forgot,
Kingston, or Ballantyne the brave,
Or Cooper of the wood and wave:
So be it, also! And may I
And all my pirates share the grave
Where these and their creations lie!

R.L.S.

Preface

WHAT a wonderful challenge. Robert Louis Stevenson lived in another age, before television and computer games, yet diversions then as now turned readers away from the adventure awaiting them in the pages of a book. The author of *Treasure Island* knew that to reject his tales of grand adventure would be to reject the challenge of adventure itself. For who hasn't dreamed of finding a chest of buried pirate loot, of sailing off, kidnapped, aboard a pirate brig, of skirmishes on the Spanish Main?

I have lived some of that grand adventure—challenged by the sea, haunted by the mysteries of the oceans, charmed by the dwellers of the deep. I have been swimming with dolphins, perhaps the only dolphins in the world trained to use their echolocation to find treasure buried beneath the sand underwater. I have shared the exploits of those who have said their lives will be different, who have embarked on voyages of exploration, who have searched in quest of treasure. Many have failed, but some have met the challenge and found great wealth.

Putting out to sea is a part of the challenge, pitting sturdy seafarers against the elements of nature. The conquest of human fear and superstition, ignorance and crude navigational technology put explorers upon the sea to reach out, to challenge the vast unknown, to discover the New World, to explore and eventually conquer the terrestrial planet. For many challengers, the oceans consumed them, destroying their feeble ships: drowned souls lost overboard, ships and fleets dashed against the shoals and shores of time. These memorials to history lost are being found again by new ocean explorers.

We will voyage from place to place, discovering the sunken land, exploring bits of history under the sea. With each shipwreck, a piece of life was lost, but in a way, also

Gold coins found on the shipwrecks of the lost 1707 fleet on Scilly.

conserved in the artifacts and personal effects of people who lived then.

We will unravel the mysteries of undersea discovery, prowl the back bays and harbors in quest of our maritime heritage and open cargoes sealed in their watery graves twenty-two hundred years earlier.

We will ship out together on this voyage under the sea, challenged by the past as adventurers of old were challenged by the future. We will swim among ghost fleets and phantom ships, prowl coves and beaches, interview old and young witnesses to great tragedy and high adventure. We will run before the wind to the place where Robert Louis Stevenson and the crew of *Treasure Island* braved "Storm and adventure, heat and cold . . . schooners, islands and maroons, And Buccaneers and buried Gold."

The hidden reef in Anegada. It extends many miles into the passage between the Caribbean and Atlantic, luring ships to wreck on the shallow shoals and reefs just under the surface.

1   The Sunken Land

THE reef extends thirteen miles into the Anegada Passage. It was called Anegada by Christopher Columbus, who explored what is now the British Virgin Islands during his second voyage of discovery in 1493. The name means the sunken land. This fifteen-mile-long flat island with its treacherous coral reef is barely visible to mariners until they are almost upon it. Since the Anegada Passage is an important pass between the Atlantic Ocean and the Caribbean Sea, the reef around Anegada has claimed hundreds of ships, wrecked upon the shoals and coral.

The oldest resident of Anegada is James Wallace Vanterpool. He is the grandson of a Dutch sailor who shipwrecked on the island, married a local woman and stayed on. At 92, Uncle Wallace, as everybody calls him out of fondness and respect, remembers clearly the days when wrecking was an important occupation on Anegada. He is quick to point out that the Anegadians would first be sure the crews of the wrecked ships were taken to safety before the wreckers went to see what was to be had on the derelict ships.

Uncle Wallace tells wonderful stories about young residents on the island finding

great wealth, diving the wrecked ships, although he was not permitted to go out himself until he was twelve or fourteen.

On one particular wreck the young men recovered so many gold doubloons that they saved them in a pail. When the young divers got ready to share their find, Uncle Wallace recounts, they ladled the gold coins out in a scoop, each in turn taking a dip from the pail of gold.

He tells another story about a ship they called the perfume wreck. It was an iron steam vessel, the *Ida*, bound from Spain to Puerto Rico with a general cargo on board. Bales of cloth washed up on shore from the

Uncle Wallace, a wrecker in his day, the grandson of a shipwrecked Dutch sailor. When he was a youth, boys scooped out doubloons of gold from sunken galleons.

wreck, still bound around with iron bands. Uncle Wallace remembers people from the village going down to the bay, and chopping the iron bands away so they could get at the cloth. The bay smelled sweet for weeks after the ship went down, Uncle Wallace recounts, as her cargo of perfume spilled into the water.

A spot on Anegada still recalls a squabble between two friends over a treasure they dove out of one of the wrecks. As Uncle Wallace tells the story, two young friends found a table made of pure gold while diving. When they got it to shore they began arguing over who owned the table. The argument grew heated, until one of the young men threw the table into a salt pond to end the dispute. To this day the place is called Gold Table Pond.

When he was younger, Uncle Wallace guided many people out to the shipwrecks. One of the men he guided has become something of a legendary figure himself.

Living on his own private island, Bert Kilbride and his clan charter their boat, taking tourists out diving. Some of the shipwreck sites Bert was shown by Uncle Wallace are now being explored by an archaeological venture Bert founded with other treasure hunters. They eventually hope to recover treasure galleons and pirate ships that were recorded sunk on Anegada's reef.

One of Bert Kilbride's favorite wrecks lies off Salt Island. Sunk in a violent hurricane in 1867, the iron-hulled Royal Mail Steamer *Rhone* was one of the proudest and most modern ships of her day. The *Rhone* lay at anchor with her sister ship the *Conway*. All

of a sudden the barometer fell, warning of a storm. The sky darkened and the violent fury of the wind began to batter the ships. The *Conway* transferred her passengers to the larger ship and pulled up anchor. As the seas grew worse the *Rhone*'s captain decided to weigh anchor and try to outrun the storm. Just as the ship was about to round the point of Salt Island, making for the shelter of Road Town Harbor, a strong gust of wind caught it and dashed the iron steamer against the rocks, breaking it in two.

Most of the passengers and crew perished aboard the 331-foot-long *Rhone,* and her

Bert Kilbride, who is exploring the shipwrecks of Anegada, posing by a treasure chest and the skull and bones of the ship's carpenter from the sunken vessel Rhone.

cargo was lost. Years later, Bert Kilbride swam inside the wreckage and recovered ship's china and assorted gear. Deep inside the wreck, Bert came upon the skeletal remains of one of the *Rhone*'s ill-fated crewmen. Reaching down into the silt, Bert felt the remnants of the crewman's shirt. In the pocket he found a small snuffbox with the name Steve Kenyon engraved on it. Bert found the ship's manifest and crew list in a forgotten archive and discovered that he had come upon the remains of the ship's carpenter.

Bert Kilbride and the archaeological venture workers calculate that there is about 400 to 600 million dollars in treasure in waters around the British Virgin Islands. One of the treasure ships they hope to locate is the *San Ignacio*, which sank in 1742 bearing a cargo of gold. The *San Ignacio* was owned by the Company of Caracas, a private company licensed by Spain to do business in the Indies in 1700. The *San Ignacio*'s manifests show that the vessel sank with several hundred tons of products aboard including gold and uncut diamonds.

Archaeologist drawing and studying artifacts found below.

Two other rich treasure ships, the *Soledad* and the *San Antonio* are also rumored to have gone down in the shallow water somewhere along Anegada's thirteen-mile-long Horseshoe Reef.

One of the wrecks being sought by the divers is the *Defiance*. The *Defiance* was captained by the privateer Prince Maurice, who with his brother, the notorious privateer admiral Prince Rupert, plied the waters around the Virgin Islands, taking prizes and booty. Bert thinks they've located the *Defiance*, which was carrying gold and emeralds when it sank in 1652. Bert has dated the artifacts he recovered on the site to the 1652 shipwreck, but thinks two more ships went down directly on top of where the *Defiance* is resting, making its recovery more difficult.

In 1967, Bert Kilbride was appointed official Receiver of the wreck of the Royal Navy ship, H.M.S. *Astrea*. The *Astrea* was a thirty-two-gun frigate that struck Anegada's reef in 1808. When the weather worsened, the captain ordered the *Astrea* abandoned. The ship sank outside the reef and was broken up by hurricanes and storms.

Diver George Marler and his wife Luana have spent many hours exploring the wreck of the *Astrea*, diving down between huge valleys in the reef to explore the ship's cannons and huge anchors. George Marler fans sand out of small potholes in the reef, discovering musket balls and shot, small brass nails and ship's fittings which once adorned the *Astrea*.

There is a longtime friendship between the Marlers and Kilbrides, but also a friendly rivalry as to who has found the most exciting artifacts from the island's ship-

Lou and George Marler (Lou middle, George in striped shirt) examining tiny cut glass cup and saucer found on Anegada wreck.

The cup and saucer with slave trade beads and musket balls.

wrecks. Bert invited the Marlers to dinner on his private island one night and served a delicious meal on china plates he recovered from the wreck of the *Rhone*. Not one to be outdone, George Marler insists that he is going to reciprocate Bert's hospitality, but intends to set Bert's place with *Rhone* china marked "Second Class."

China from the wreck of the Rhone.

It is rumored that the infamous pirate Blackbeard plied these waters of the Anegada Passage, and other pirates plagued merchant shipping, putting lanterns along the beach to lure unsuspecting ships close to the treacherous shoals to wreck, then pouncing on them to steal the cargo.

One thing Uncle Wallace is sure of,

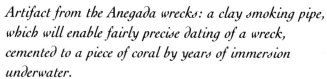

Artifact from the Anegada wrecks: a clay smoking pipe, which will enable fairly precise dating of a wreck, cemented to a piece of coral by years of immersion underwater.

Flintlock pistol recovered from a galleon sunk on Anegada with the piece of flint still in place, ready for action.

Cannons from shipwreck on Anegada.

Anegada has plenty of shipwrecks. Even today, ships continue to wreck on the dangerous shoals and Anegadians take to their boats to rescue the crews.

Lowell Wheatley, who with his wife, Vivian, owns Anegada's only hotel, recently rescued the crew of the freighter *Ada 1*. The ship lost its rudder, and before the crew could get it fixed, they ran up on the reef and couldn't get off. As a reward for rescuing the captain and crew of six and their two dogs, Lowell was allowed to take the ship's large brass compass and binnacle, wheel, telegraph and brass foghorn, which now decorates the dining room of his hotel.

Author John Christopher Fine with some not-so-old artifacts recovered from British Virgin Islands shipwreck.

The shipwrecks of Anegada will continue to lure adventurers and treasure hunters to the islands in search of great fortunes. Some, like the legendary Anegadians of old, will be lucky enough to find gold. Others will just have to make do with a musket ball and an exciting dive into the history of the sunken land.

Diver with grid used to study and record archaeological data underwater.

2   Spain's Lost Treasure Fleet

WHILE Anegada played host to historic ships that wrecked upon its shores, elsewhere in the Caribbean, Mexico, South and Central America, events were taking place during the conquest of the New World that would make an impact hundreds of years later.

The Spanish had conquered the Inca and Aztec civilizations in the Americas, enslaving peoples whose advanced culture is only now being rediscovered. It was greed, the pursuit of gold and silver, pearls and emeralds, that lured the Spaniards in their quest. Each year they carried treasure back to Spain aboard heavily guarded plate fleets. What they couldn't guard against were the fierce storms of the tropical Atlantic Ocean.

Almost three hundred fifty years later, young men would locate evidence of some of Spain's lost treasure galleons. The true tale of this discovery is as adventurous as any mystery novel ever imagined. Sixty million dollars' worth of treasure has been brought up from one site and Spanish archives log some 360 million dollars' worth of treasure remaining among the as yet undiscovered wreckage of these lost ships. Here is the tale of high adventure and treasure found.

KEVIN'S father was one of the first divers in the Florida Keys. He had worked in a

Gold doubloon found on the Spanish galleons.

Diver Tom Ford with gold bar and disk recovered underwater.

hard hat rig, building and repairing the bridges that eventually formed the modern highway system from Miami to Key West. It was almost by accident that Art McKee found the legendary lost treasure fleet that sank off the Florida Keys in 1733.

Kevin's first expedition with his father came when he was just nineteen years old. Art was having problems with his health and Kevin went along to help with the diving. Turtle hunters had reported finding gold and silver from a galleon on a shallow reef. Kevin and his father found the spot where the treasure galleon had supposedly wrecked, but the ship had long since been

Kevin McKee proudly posing with photo of his dad in the hard hat gear he used in the forties, diving for a living, then treasure hunting.

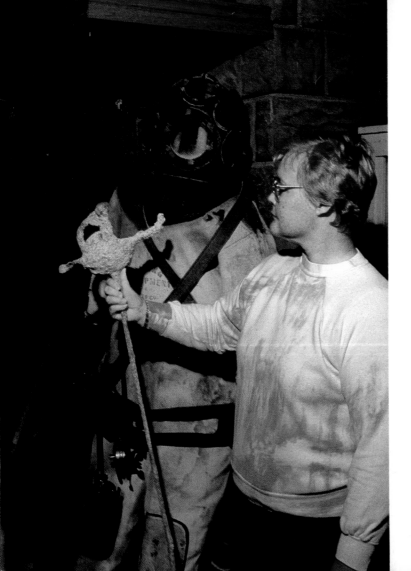

overgrown by coral. They didn't have the proper tools aboard to get under the coral. As Kevin tells it, the crew was untested; his father chartered the boat without knowing the captain. When they found the wreck, the captain suggested sailing into port to get primer cord to blast the reef apart to get at the treasure.

Art had a sixth sense about trouble. He had seen the effects of treasure fever before. Art knew that if they made port the captain and crew would try to file a claim on the wreck for themselves. Finally, according to Kevin, somebody sabotaged their diving compressor and they had to give up the

Jean McKee, widow of the late Art McKee, the father of modern treasure diving, holding rapier Art found off Florida's coast.

search. Kevin was never able to get back with his father to the mystery galleon. His dad's health got worse and Art McKee died.

Recently dismantling the treasure museum his father and mother built in the Florida Keys, Kevin admitted that he was bitten by the treasure bug. Kevin McKee intends to follow in his father's footsteps and seek his fortune, hoping to find treasure wrecks buried off the coast.

Pointing to an old pirate chest, Kevin describes how a beachcomber said he found the chest and offered it for sale to his father. The chest was empty then, in spite of a secret lock, but a year later, the once penniless beachcomber opened a hotel and restaurant.

The trick lock on Kevin McKee's treasure chest, a pirate chest.

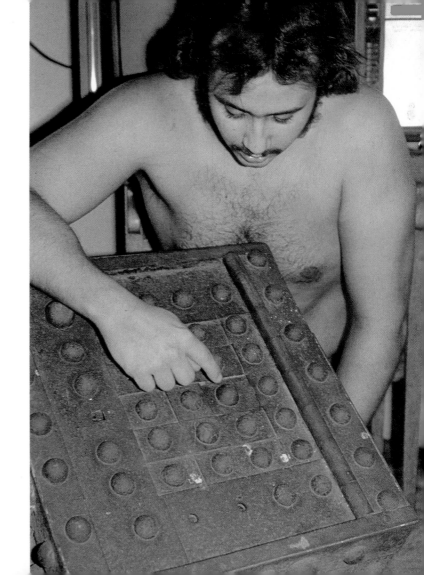

Art McKee bought the old pirate chest and Kevin wonders what was in the heavy iron box the family still keeps in their living room.

Fine Ming porcelain from China, found in the Spanish galleons, came overland on the backs of Indian slaves to be loaded aboard the annual Spanish treasure fleets, homeward bound from the New World. The Spanish had "Manila" galleons, which traded with China.

Many of the old shipwrecks Art McKee found were time capsules, their cargoes and stores, provisions, tools, navigational instruments and riches buried under 350 years of coral growth.

One of the most fascinating was discovered quite by accident. The divers recovered two cannons, crossed and cemented together by years of coral growth. The wreck was the H.M.S. *Winchester,* a British warship that sank on the reef near Plantation Key in 1695. When Art got the cannons ashore and pried them apart, they found a seaman's prayer book with parts of the pages still legible. The prayer book must have become wedged between the crossed cannons when the *Winchester* sank and was preserved by the eventual growth around them. Only one's imagination can explain

how the prayer book got there, perhaps held by a sailor in the last minutes before the violence of the hurricane dashed his ship upon the reef.

KEVIN'S sister Karen works with Mel Fisher, a famous treasure hunter in Key West, Florida. Kevin also dives with the Fishers when he gets time, working with them to excavate the richest treasure galleons ever found underwater.

Mel Fisher and his family share a dream of finding treasure that began more than a dozen years ago. When the Fishers first came to the Florida Keys, they stopped in to

Part of a Bible found preserved between two crossed cannons on a shipwreck off Florida's coast by Art McKee.

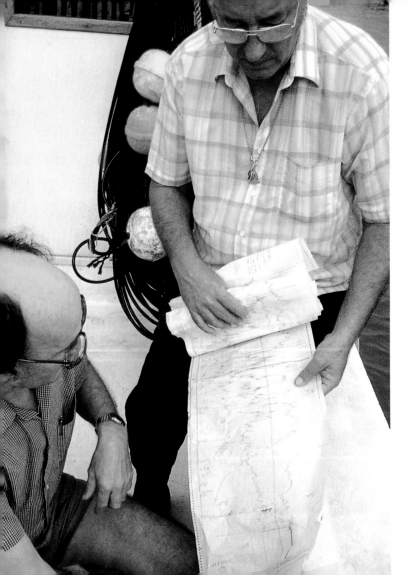

see Art and Jean McKee in Tavernier. Mel was fascinated by the stories Art told and the priceless treasures he had recovered from the Florida wrecks. The men struck up a friendship and collaborated from time to time in treasure-hunting. Art continued to work his underwater sites while Mel Fisher was intent on living out his lifelong fantasy of really striking it rich.

Fisher and his family had mentally staked claim to two elusive treasure galleons: The *Nuestra Señora de Atocha* and the *Santa Margarita*, sunk in 1622 in a hurricane off the Marquesas Islands, forty miles south of Key West. The legendary galleons were said to

Mel Fisher (plaid shirt) with Fay Field examining charts of a new invention to locate treasure underwater. Mel calls it his Squirkometer.

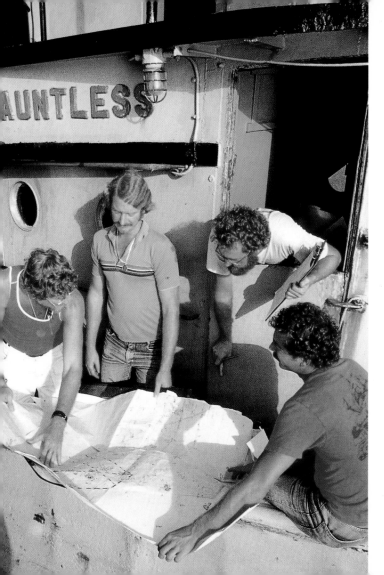

Duncan, Mel's son, Tom and Andy plan a treasure dive.

contain half a billion dollars worth of gold, silver, jewels and precious wares from the Spanish conquest of the New World.

The Plate Fleet of 1622 contained the entire year's output from the great silver mine at Potosi and the entire output of the mint in Mexico City. Heavily laden with gold and silver, the treasure fleet put out for the long trip back to Spain. Only a day's sail out of Havana, the fleet was put upon by the fury of a hurricane. The *Atocha* struck the shoals and was ripped open, strewing her valuable cargo over the bottom. The galleon *Santa Margarita* sank within sight of the *Atocha*. With their sinking, the hopes of King Philip IV of Spain and a powerful merchant community were dashed. Spain eventually commissioned Don Francisco Nuñez Melián to salvage what he could of the treasure fleet. Using primitive diving techniques, Melián did succeed in rescuing some of the treasure, eventually giving up as Spain's enemies and pirates endangered their presence in Caribbean waters.

Hundreds of years later, Mel Fisher persisted in his search for the shipwrecks, using modern electronic equipment. Diving over the probable wreck site, Mel's oldest son Dirk located an anchor, then cannons belonging to the *Atocha*. When news of the find got out, world attention was drawn to south Florida and the exploits of this remarkable family.

The cannons were what salvors or treasure hunters call provenance: something that enables archaeologists and historians to authenticate a find and identify its origin. Silver bars weighing seventy-four pounds each were also found on the site. Numbers on the bars matched the *Atocha*'s manifest in the Spanish archives. The ship the Fishers found was definitely the treasure galleon *Atocha*.

In the midst of celebrating what was for the Fishers the greatest event in their lives, after years of searching, a tragic accident at sea dashed the families' hopes.

A tugboat the Fishers bought for the salvage operation capsized. Mel's son Dirk, Dirk's wife and a young diver were trapped inside and drowned.

James Sinclair prepares a reverse electrolysis bath to clean silver pieces of eight.

The coins in the bath.

After the funeral, the Fisher family decided that Dirk would have wanted them to push on. With heavy hearts, the Fisher clan continued to work on the site, eventually coming across the remains of the second galleon, the *Santa Margarita*.

The Fishers' persistence paid off. Recently Mel and his divers hit a pocket of silver bars and coins from the *Atocha* wreck site. Each of the more than two hundred silver bars recovered weighed about seventy-four pounds and divers were also bringing up huge clumps of silver pieces of eight.

When the ships hit the reefs and shoals, the force of the hurricane broke them up, scattering their treasure over miles and miles of ocean. This has made the treasure hunt more difficult, almost like searching for a needle in a haystack.

Mel Fisher estimates that to date he and his team of divers have recovered about 60 million dollars' worth of treasure from the two shipwrecks.

The motto that is scrawled almost everywhere around Fisher's dock and boats, made famous by the Fisher clan, exemplifies the spirit of these never-give-in adventurers.

Mel Fisher's divers keeping tally of the valuable finds.

"Today's the day," is this Key West treasure hunter's slogan, and with almost a half-billion dollars' worth of gold and silver still in the offing, Mel's continuing challenge of the sea will almost surely be answered with more riches.

Emerald cross recovered by Mel Fisher. The ensemble, with a man's emerald ring and the silver box in which it was found, is worth $750,000.

3   Pucker and the Silver Bar

SOMEWHERE along this treasure route from the New World, up through the Straits of Florida, navigating the Gulf Stream, then out past Bermuda and back to Europe, many vessels were lost. Others were plundered by pirates and privateers. Pucker Scott is on the trail of one such lost treasure. Using a metal detector, he has already found cob coins and a silver bar. This is Pucker's story of discovery on his rocky island home south of Cuba.

PUCKER lives on Brac, one of the Cayman Islands in the Caribbean Sea. His real name is Raymond Scott, but all his friends on the small island of Cayman Brac call him by his nickname. Pucker first got interested in treasure hunting after hearing tales of high adventure about pirates and treasure ships. Some of the stories had been passed on by older residents of the Brac as part of the history of their island.

Not one to be easily swayed by stories, the young man mostly just accepted the tales as folklore, until one day, after a fierce storm had raged over the island, Pucker discovered a small silver coin while walking along the beach near his home.

Pucker showed the coin to a friend, Winston McDermot, a professional charter captain who earns his living taking visitors scuba diving over the Brac's famous reefs.

Winston recognized the coin immediately. The small silver "cob" was a four *real* coin from the days of the Spanish Main. These coins, and thousands like them, were stamped out in Mexico before modern minting was invented. The coins, cut in irregular shapes from a silver bar, were called "cabo de barra" or cobs. The coins were then clipped until the proper weight was obtained. When the coin was sized and correctly weighed, it was stamped with the mint mark of the Indies and the famous Crusader's cross.

Pucker Scott (shorts) with Winston McDermot on Cayman Brac with silver bar he found.

Excited by his find, Pucker sought out older residents on the Brac to help him learn more about his island and about the pirates and ships that prowled the water around his home.

The Cayman islanders were known for great feats of bravery in the early days. Residents often risked their lives to rescue sailors shipwrecked on the reefs and treacherous shoals offshore. The people of the Caymans pay no income tax to this day, a reward granted them by King George III of England in return for the rescue in November, 1778, of the passengers and crews from a convoy of ten Jamaican merchant ships including the H.M.S. *Cordelia* which wrecked on the reef. The first ship struck the reef and

Capstan underwater on ship that struck Cayman's reef.

fired a warning cannon. The others mistook the cannon for an all clear signal and followed the unfortunate ship onto the reef.

There is also a story about how the pirate Blackbeard, whose real name was Edward Teach, hotly pursued by British navy ships, landed on the Brac to hide more than 5 million dollars' worth of treasure the pirates had stolen from shipping in the Caribbean.

As the story goes, Blackbeard landed on the island in the morning, climbed the tall limestone cliff known as the Bluff, buried his treasure and climbed down on the other side of the island. Blackbeard was spotted by the British, who shot and wounded the infamous brigand. British sailors captured Blackbeard and took him prisoner on Brac. They were never able to find the treasure he buried on the island.

Pucker heard this story about Blackbeard's treasure and began exploring some of the many caves located on the island, hoping to find where the famous pirate buried his loot.

While he has not yet succeeded in finding Blackbeard's treasure, he has found plenty of evidence of early settlement on the Brac. Digging around the foundation of an old house, long since tumbled down and grown over by tropical foliage, Pucker came upon a large copper kettle that dated back to the days of early English settlement on the islands.

Encouraged by his finds, Pucker decided to use his free time to search the beach near his home where he found his first silver coin. Seeking help and advice from Winston McDermot, Pucker bought a metal detector and began combing the beach after every hurricane. He figured that was the best time to search, since the waves would wash things up from the sea and the storm would move sand and pebbles around, uncovering what was underneath.

One day, Pucker's patience was rewarded. The metal detector registered something big. Pucker began digging down in the sand, but he probed in vain. Using the metal detector again, Pucker still got a strong reading, so continued to dig. Finally, when he was down about four feet, he found an oblong shape. Pulling it out of the sand, Pucker knew he had found treasure. It was a silver bar that weighed seven and one-

Pucker and Winston with kettle and silver bar.

quarter pounds. When he sent a piece of the bar away to be assayed, Pucker found that it was pure silver.

They say there are old pirate graves on the island. Perhaps buried with the olden day buccaneers is booty from the swash-buckling era of sailing ships and treasure galleons.

Another treasure story is real enough. Winston McDermot remembers his mother telling him about seeing fishermen finding an old shipwreck on one of the reefs. The fish-ermen recovered some silver coins and showed them to his mother. From the de-scription, Winston believes that the wreck was a schooner owned by one of the Brac's more legendary figures.

Dick Sessinger was marooned on Cayman Brac in the early days, the only survivor of a

shipwreck. Sessinger lived off the land and escaped being killed by pirates who frequented the Brac to bury their loot. It is said that Sessinger would walk around backwards so the pirates wouldn't find his hideout. Eventually, Dick Sessinger became a sort of merchant, and pirates traded with him to provision their ships. Sessinger's business soon prospered and he bought a schooner. One day, as Sessinger was trying to make it through a pass in the reef, a storm came up and his schooner capsized. Sessinger survived, but a chest of silver coins sank with the ship. Winston believes that the coins his mother was shown, which the fishermen found on the reef, were from

Winston in Cayman Brac's old graveyard by the beach, where pirates were buried in olden days.

Dick Sessinger's shipwreck. Winston continues to search for the wreckage, certain that there are many more coins to be uncovered from Dick Sessinger's cache.

NOT far from the Brac is Grand Cayman Island. Here some three hundred ships have met their end, wrecked on the treacherous reef that surrounds a large part of it.

Diving with her father, Sandy Hytha enjoys exploring the shallow wrecks on Grand Cayman's East End. Schooners and frigates, merchant ships and paddle-wheelers litter the reefs, victims of storms and errors in navigation.

Sandy's father is a professional diver who makes movies for television. While her father is working underwater, Sandy enjoys snorkeling around the shipwrecks to see

how many different kinds of colorful fish she can count.

In between dives, her father, Gerry Hytha, tells stories about some of the shipwrecks. One wreck sits right up on the reef, a large hole torn through her rusted hull. Gerry explains that the wreck is the *Ridgefield*, a tramp steamer that belonged to the CIA. The *Ridgefield* was part of the flotilla that landed a secret army on Cuba in 1961, during the ill-fated Bay of Pigs invasion.

Gerry describes how the captain of the *Ridgefield*, afraid they were being chased by a Russian submarine, misjudged the location.

The CIA spy ship, the crew of which, thinking they were being pursued by a Russian submarine, hit the reef on Grand Cayman Island after the Bay of Pigs invasion.

Instead of making it through the pass to safety beyond the reef, the ship ran up on the coral, where it remains to this day, high and dry on the East End reef.

While making underwater films for kids to enjoy, Gerry and his daughter Sandy have come to appreciate the rich heritage and history of the Cayman Islands. Part of the fun is learning about the ships that have gone down on the reefs, trying to put together the puzzle of what the ships were, what they were carrying and when and how they met their watery graves.

Residents on the Caymans are friendly and proud of their island heritage. Ron Meiselman, a photographer whose son and daughter both dive, enjoys weekends aboard a runabout, taking pictures of the sunken ships. One of his favorite wrecks is the *Pal-*

Kids at play on Grand Cayman.

las, a Norwegian brigantine that ran up on the reef during a storm in 1903. Parts of the ship are still visible sticking out of the water, broken apart by the fury of the wind and sea. Huge anchors mark the spot where the captain of the *Pallas* tried, too late, to prevent his ship from crashing over the reef.

LIKE Pucker, visitors to the islands and residents alike can enjoy the excitement of beachcombing and treasure hunting in the Caymans. Even if everyone doesn't find a silver bar or handful of pirate doubloons, the treasure of the Caymans is the beautiful reef life that lives on the sunken ships. And who knows, someday a lucky snorkeler or cave explorer may just happen upon Blackbeard's long-lost pirate booty.

4   The Volcano and the French Fleet

W E'LL now move from finding treasure to exploring wrecks of ships lost in a moment of great tragedy. The tragedy also includes a remarkable story about a hapless young man whose life was saved because he was in jail. The young scoundrel was out carousing. Little did he know that being arrested for rowdiness would save his life.

Early one morning a volcano erupted with such force that an entire city of thirty thousand people was annihilated. Only the prisoner, confined in a tiny cell, survived.

Fourteen ships anchored in the bay were also destroyed. While none of these shipwrecks contained treasure, their cargoes of trade goods and building materials have been discovered right where they sank, providing interesting insight into the events surrounding the tragedy of St. Pierre.

THE story of Cyparis is almost as sensational as the event that brought him worldwide attention. On the morning of May 8, 1902, the volcano Mont-Pelée erupted on the island of Martinique in the French West

Indies. With the explosion, a large, cosmopolitan city was destroyed. Of the thirty thousand inhabitants of Saint-Pierre, only one survived. This one was Louis Cyparis. Cyparis, a prisoner in a tiny "cachot" or solitary cell, survived, but was badly burned on his face and body where the searing volcanic

Mayor of St.-Pierre showing author where shipwrecks lie.

Documentary pictures showing St.-Pierre bay with the ships lined up and the immediate aftermath of the eruption of Mt.-Pelée,

dust managed to blow through a slit in the wall. It was fate alone that saved Cyparis, an islander who had been arrested for fighting and being drunk and disorderly. There being a festival in a nearby town, Cyparis walked away from his jail sentence to enjoy the gala celebration. When the party was over and Cyparis woke up the next morn-

one, were sunk, in an event unique in the annals of maritime history.

The commander of the one ship that got away only barely managed to save it. His ship, the *Roddam*, a large vessel of the Quebec Line, was set on fire and badly damaged. Many of the crew members were killed or injured.

The only survivor of the tragic eruption of Mt.-Pelee was Cyparis, imprisoned in this tiny cell, or cachot!

ing, he went back to Saint-Pierre, where his jailers confined him for added punishment in the little solitary cell that saved his life. After the eruption, P. T. Barnum hired Cyparis, who toured with the circus until his death.

For the fourteen ships riding at anchor in the Bay of Saint-Pierre, the tragic eruption afforded no escape. All of the ships, save

The drama of the *Roddam*'s ordeal at sea, as the crew struggled to steam out of the Bay of Saint-Pierre, can only be imagined from the captain's report. When they reached the safety of the neighboring island of Saint Lucia, some twenty-five miles away, the captain had to wait for three days until first the fires aboard his ship were put out and then until the volcanic ash and dust piled on the *Roddam*'s decks cooled down sufficiently to be removed. It required six barge loads to cart the ashes away, since port authorities refused to allow it to be dumped in the harbor. Each barge contained twenty tons. The burning cinders on the *Roddam*'s decks alone weighed one hundred twenty tons.

The thirteen other ships lined up at anchor did not fare as well as the *Roddam*. Her sister ship, the iron Quebec Liner *Roraima*, became a death trap for her crew and passengers when the searing heat set fire to her cargo. The massive iron steamship burned for three days before sinking in deep water.

Because of its depth, divers using scuba tanks have little time to explore the wreck of the *Roraima* before having to head back to the surface to avoid the dreaded diving disease known as the bends. Swimming back to the surface, divers must ascend slowly and wait at prescribed decompression stops on the way up to allow the nitrogen that has saturated their blood and tissues to leave their system as gas when they breathe.

The *Roraima* has huge cargo holds, deep

The ladder, at fifty-four meters deep, leading down into Roraima*'s hold.*

and dark, where even the strong underwater lamps divers use appear only as thin pencils of light. The catwalks are deserted and eerie, rust brown with long strands of black wire coral growing up from them.

The rest of the ships that went down when Mont-Pelée erupted were wooden sailing vessels, merchant ships with cargoes of building materials, clothing and assorted trade goods. The ships are like time capsules, each preserving a way of life in 1902. On the wooden sailing vessel *Gabrielle,* wine bottles were found, some with their contents still inside. The wine has turned to vinegar after all the years under the sea, much to the dismay of French divers in the area. The captain of the *Gabrielle* seemed to have refined tastes, judging from the beautiful china cups and dishes found in the area that once

Author John Fine (red trunks) with Michel Metery with artifacts found on St.-Pierre shipwrecks.

served as the ship's pantry. Michel Metery, the manager of Martinique's Latitude Hotel, has, over the years, become an expert on the shipwrecks in Saint-Pierre Bay and he has found beautiful examples of glassware on the *Gabrielle.*

The wooden planks of the *Gabrielle* were fastened in the old-fashioned way with copper and brass nails that wouldn't rust. But, the wood, like that of most of the ships, has rotted with the passage of time.

Some of the vessels stick only a few feet out of the sand. Divers looking for remnants of their cargo often gently fan away the sand with their hands. Fanning in one section of the *Gabrielle*, Michel Metery found human bones, solemn evidence of the tragedy that befell her crew.

On the wreck of the *Teresa Lovico*, molded cylinders stick up from the remnants of her deck. On close inspection divers can see that the oblong shapes are cement hardened permanently in the shape of the wooden barrels that held it, deck cargo when the *Lovico* sank. Tiles and coils of rope prove that the ship was unloading building materials when the volcano erupted.

The disaster of Mont-Pelée's eruption was compared to the eruption of Mount Vesuvius in A.D. 79, which destroyed the cities of Pompeii and Herculaneum. Like Pompeii, historians and archaeologists have culled valuable information about a civilization buried intact by a holocaust.

Before the eruption, the city of Saint-Pierre was regarded as the gem of the Caribbean, complete with a majestic cathedral and opera house. The port of Saint-Pierre bustled with trade. The year 1902 was one of transition from sail to steam power.

Diving with Michel Metery is a rewarding voyage into this history of the West Indies. The fourteen ships that met their fate in Saint-Pierre are now underwater memorials to the development of commerce, museums that afford exciting adventures into another time, another era, a day when, for the people of Saint-Pierre, the world stood still.

View of St.-Pierre today.

5 Ancient Shipwrecks in the Mediterranean

To FIND something underwater that hasn't been seen or touched by a human hand in over two thousand years is a great thrill. Discovering the history of Greek and Roman occupation by exploring and excavating sunken ships is a great adventure. We'll travel to the Mediterranean Sea, the place where Western civilization was born and where underwater exploration is slowly aiding its rediscovery.

WHEN a friend and fellow diver became quite secretive and disappeared with the boat every afternoon, we became suspicious. One day we decided to investigate and climbed a hill overlooking the sea to watch him. Our friend took off alone as usual and pulled the boat into a small bay down the coast. That was it, we thought, he had found something valuable and was busy digging it up.

AT the height of its power, the ancient Roman Empire stretched over most of Europe. What is now Spain was part of their empire, with many Roman trading cities established

Mediterranean shipwreck site showing scattered pottery and amphora shards off Spanish coast dating to second century BC.

Site off the Spanish coast of author's early shipwreck.

along the Mediterranean coast. The ancient Roman city of Ampurias was only a short distance by sea from the spot where our diver friend was secretly digging.

Once confronted with our observations, the diver confessed that he had stumbled upon a Roman shipwreck, which he suspected sank before the birth of Christ. The diver had been digging by hand and had moved as much sand as he could alone, so welcomed additional help.

Mounting a water jet on a small boat, we set off to try to identify the wreck our companion had found. A water jet is nothing more than a water hose powered by a portable compressor. Underwater, the stream of water blows away debris over a wreck site. Underwater excavation tools like the water jet must be used with care because they can damage or blow away delicate artifacts or small coins. But by using the water jet carefully, our team of divers could then uncover amphorae and other pottery jars.

Amphorae are graceful ceramic jars that were used in the same way barrels or drums are today. In them wine, olive oil and other foodstuffs were transported. The insides of the amphorae were coated with pine pitch to make them waterproof, and they were sealed at the neck with stoppers and wax.

From excavations on land, archaeologists have developed amphorae identification into an exacting science, making it possible to date the pottery containers and tell where they originated by their distinctive shape, and the shape of the neck, lip and handles. Some jars even bear marks of the merchant who owned them. Amphorae were carried as deck cargo on early Greek and Roman ships, arranged in rows and packed in straw to keep them from breaking on the voyage.

Diving on the site, one of the divers dis-

Diver bringing up amphora.

lodged a boulder. Behind it we could feel the shape of an amphora still buried in the mud. Using the water jet carefully, we slowly loosened the amphora and pulled it free. It was a beautiful example. While some of the divers struggled with the large amphora, bringing it up to the dive boat, we continued to dig in the area excavated by the water jet. Small pottery jars and vases turned up, along with heavy material fused together and covered by marine growth.

Once back on shore, we carefully broke the mass of fused material apart. Inside, there were pieces from the ship's navigational instruments and a pointed lead plumb bob, some nails and small metal objects.

Near the site, one of our companions found a jas. In Roman times, anchors were cast in lead with a wooden stock. After years underwater, the wood rots away, so that all that remains is the heavy cast lead portion called the jas.

Taking all of our artifacts together, we began measuring and studying, comparing what we found with books and research materials about shipwrecks. From the amphora

recovered we were able to date the wreck to about the second century before the birth of Christ. There were many different types of amphorae on the ship, so we concluded that it was a merchant trader that must have made several stops along the route to trade, picking up and discharging cargo from many ports.

A coral diver, diving very deep off the tip of a rock called the Maza d'Oro near Cabo Creus, not far from where we had excavated the first shipwreck, found another. This ship had gone down in very deep water, almost 240 feet. The depth of this wreck meant that divers would have only ten or fifteen minutes to work on the site before having to come back to shallow water under the diving

Amphora aboard.

boat and decompress before being able to surface. The depth also meant that the compressed air divers used in the scuba tanks would not last very long. When diving deep on compressed air, nitrogen dissolved in the blood causes disorientation, known as nitrogen narcosis or rapture of the deep.

The coral diver reported that the shipwreck was almost intact. Of course the exposed parts of the wood had long since rotted away, but the amphorae were arranged neatly in rows, untouched by other divers. It was an exciting discovery.

On our first dive over the wreck I took two cameras and an underwater strobe light to photograph the ship. As we dove down and my depth meter registered 150 feet, I began to feel the telling effects of nitrogen narcosis. Knowing what the warning signs

Jas, or early lead anchors.

are, an experienced diver can stay in control. At the bottom, the extreme pressure jammed one of my cameras. Luckily, the other worked, and we began taking pictures of the wreckage.

There was a large lead jas from the anchor. It measured about five feet long. The hole in the middle where the wooden stock once was fixed was empty. Nearby, rows of amphorae were laid out. Small olive jars and pottery were found in the mud under the amphorae.

Almost before we realized it, our time on the wreck was over and we had to surface. The ten minutes below meant that we would have to take twenty-three minutes to surface, stopping and waiting at the different depths indicated by our decompression tables.

While many fabled wrecks offer the lure of gold and treasure, the artifacts that we were able to photograph and study on these Roman shipwrecks were in many ways more exciting. To touch an object that was used for the last time 2,200 years ago is a thrilling experience. The research taught us many lessons about how the Romans lived and how they traded along the Mediterranean coast.

For us and the archaeological divers who followed, these shipwrecks were truly exciting discoveries of early Roman civilization.

VILLEFRANCHE sur Mer is a small port on the Mediterranean just a few miles south of Nice along the fabled French Riviera. A popular tourist spot in summer, Villefranche's beautiful sprawling bay provided sheltered harbor and safe anchorage to ships throughout history.

The French *Groupe de Recherche en Archeologie Navale,* or Naval Archaeological Research Group, working under the direction of Commander Philippe Tailliez and French Navy Captain Max Guerout, with young volunteers, have been excavating and studying a rare example of a carack that sank in the harbor around 1475, in about sixty feet of water.

Not much is known about the ship thus far except that it was an armed merchant vessel. The cannons aboard were not cast; rather they are tubes wrapped with wire that fired stone cannon balls. Each of the projec-

Max Guerout briefing youthful divers at Villefranche.

tiles was chiseled by hand, made perfectly round, from a single piece of granite.

GRAN volunteers like Marion Delhaye, Karine Malcor, Alexis Kourtessis, Erwann Marechal, Stephane Legranché, Eric Farrugia and others spend their summer holiday diving with French naval personnel and marine archaeologists to first delicately uncover the wooden remnants of the ship from a

Diver underwater at Villefranche operating airlift to expose wreckage and find small artifacts.

Divers measuring a delicate scoop found amid the Villefranche wreckage.

deep covering of sand, silt and gravel, then excavate the delicate parts of the ship which are brought to the surface for study and conservation.

Very few coins were found on the shipwreck, which was obviously pillaged over the years by local divers. One of the coins recovered by Captain Max Guerout is a Maria Sforza Italian lire dated 1475. This coin enabled an approximate dating of the shipwreck. It turned out that the coin was the first Italian lire used as money, a sign of advancement in commerce and the emergence from the Middle Ages. Other coins found were tokens or trade pieces. Captain Guerout and his young team of volunteers have recovered many pieces of pottery

Young diver filling tank at Villefranche.

which will enable archaeologists to eventually describe the origin of the ship and gain insight into an era of history along the coast.

Diver checking in, noting his bottom time.

6 The Ghost Fleet of Truk Lagoon

WAR has always provided divers with wreckage to explore. After the Japanese sneak attack on Pearl Harbor, American forces in the Pacific waited for the day they could retaliate. The opportunity to launch an attack on the heavily fortified islands of Micronesia in the South Pacific Ocean, gave the Americans a chance for revenge. The Japanese used Truk Island's deep lagoon as an anchorage for their ships. In one swoop, American planes, launched from aircraft carriers, struck at the Japanese fleet lying at anchor here, sinking scores of ships.

The Ghost Navy of Truk Lagoon remains today as an underwater park. Huge ships of war are now memorials to nature's balm, overgrown with coral and inhabited by fish. We'll explore the largest navy that never sails, the Ghost Fleet of Truk Lagoon.

HE sat on the ground under a shed out of the sun pounding breadfruit with a stone. His wife sat with him, helping with the work. For James Sellem and his wife Niku, World War II was a long time ago.

As he spoke about his experiences during the war, James Sellem pointed out toward the lagoon where a mast was sticking out of the water. He described how American planes flew over Dublon Island, dropping bombs and torpedoes on the Japanese fleet, which lay at anchor.

Lying 1,842 nautical miles southeast of Tokyo and 3,075 nautical miles southwest of Pearl Harbor, Hawaii, the peaceful islands in Micronesia became staging areas for Japan's war offensive in the Pacific. After World War I, Japan was granted a mandate over the islands in Micronesia by the League of Nations as a reward for siding with the allies against Germany. Secretly, and in violation of the League mandate, Japan began fortifying them in preparation for war. Airstrips were built, gun implacements constructed, cement bunkers, tunnels and caves cut into the mountains. As Japan prepared

Niku and James Sellem were eyewitnesses to the attack.

for an assault on Pearl Harbor, their naval forces moved into Truk, warships and supply vessels ready for their push across the Pacific.

Truk is a natural lagoon, protected by a surrounding coral reef. Inside the lagoon

there are eleven major islands and many smaller ones, some not inhabited. The forty-mile-wide lagoon, with only a few passes through the coral reef, provided a natural shelter for the Japanese fleet.

On the morning of February 17, 1944, there were almost sixty Japanese ships anchored inside the lagoon. Vice Admiral R.A. Spruance had received aerial reconnaisance pictures of the anchorage. Early in the morning, with United States aircraft carriers and warships only ninety miles northeast of Truk, Admiral Spruance ordered the attack.

The Japanese had 365 planes based on Truk. In the first hours of the fighting some 250 were destroyed. Many of the Japanese

Machine gun overgrown with coral inside Japanese airplane on the bottom of Truk Lagoon.

Documentary photo showing the ships on fire and sinking in Truk.

planes sent to intercept the Americans were shot down over the water and also crashed into the lagoon. The fierce battle over Truk lasted two days. When the battle was over, some fifty ships were sunk and lay on the bottom.

One of these ships, the *Fujikawa Maru*, an immense armed cargo ship, was hit with a torpedo and sank not far from James Sellem's home on Dublon Island. Pointing to the mast still sticking up out of the water, James motioned to show how the airplanes flew in to attack. James and his wife Niku saw the torpedo hit the *Fujikawa* and explode. Diving on the shipwreck, a cameraman for *National Geographic* remarked that nature had turned her "guns into garlands."

The *Fujikawa Maru* rests upright on the bottom. Her large forward and aft guns are overgrown with coral, sponges and rooster comb oysters. The bridge and catwalks are silent, patrolled only by fish. Large tiled bathtubs were apparently used by the Japanese crew as steam rooms. Visibility in Truk Lagoon often exceeds 100 feet, so div-

Japanese Zero fighter plane, wings folded, brand new, never used, in the hold of sunken freighter.

ers standing on the bridge of the *Fujikawa* can almost imagine the ship underway.

The *Fujikawa Maru* was being used by the Japanese as a transport ship for new airplanes. In her holds the new Japanese Zeros lie helter-skelter, stacks of propeller blades and spare parts piled nearby, silent memorials to battles never fought.

The 500-foot-long oil tanker, *Shinkoku Maru,* is another city under the sea. The dispensary of the huge ship is equipped with a sterilizer and operating table. Fine china dishes and cut crystal remain on a serving tray in what must have been the officers' dining area. On the bridge the ship's telegraphs, the system that enabled the captain to signal speed changes to the engine room, are encrusted with coral and brightly colored sponges. Her compass, still intact, points in a direction heading nowhere.

Deep in the motor spaces of the enormous ship, divers can see the skeletal remains of hapless Japanese sailors who were trapped at their posts when the ship was hit and went down.

Snorkeling with just mask and fins, divers can explore the wreck of the *Dai Na Hino Maru.* The ship's name in English means "Circle of the Sun." It was sunk in very shallow water near Uman island. The *Dai Na Hino* was a small 190-foot-long armed cargo ship. Her bow rises near the surface. Divers pose with the gun for underwater

Diver with skull found inside sunken Japanese ship in Truk.

pictures, pretending to fire the long-silenced reminder of the war.

One of the most intriguing wrecks in Truk Lagoon is the I-169 submarine. The sub submerged on April 2, 1944, warned of another impending American air attack. In their haste, the crew left open a ventilating tube and the submarine flooded and sank to the bottom. Saved for the moment by water-tight doors, the crew was able to respond to rescue divers by hammering on the hull. The Japanese tried to hoist the submarine to the surface, but failed. Eventually, the signals from the crew trapped inside the submarine stopped and the eighty-seven crewmen suffocated in their doomed ship, 140 feet below the surface.

Diving over the I-169 with Kimiou Aisek, one of Truk's best-known wreck divers and

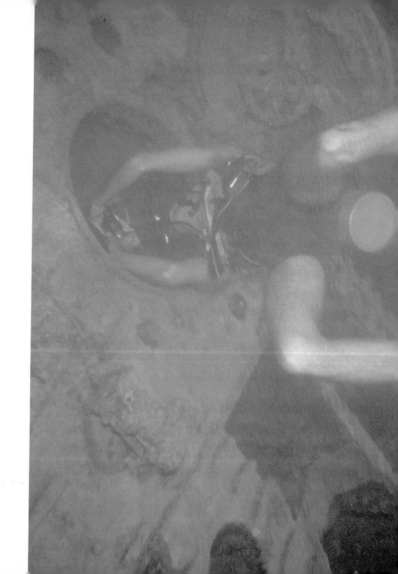

Watertight hatchway of sunken submarine.

Author entering the Japanese sub.

guides, we explored the remains of the hull. Failing in their attempt to rescue the sub, the Japanese depth charged it themselves to prevent it from falling into enemy hands.

The sub's forward area is completely destroyed. It remains intact from an area behind the conning tower to the aft torpedo tubes.

Long strands of wire coral grow up from the submarine's pressure hull, and her deck is patrolled by schools of reef fish. In a joint project, Japanese and American divers recently penetrated the submarine and removed the remains of some of the crewmen who had been trapped inside. In a solemn ceremony, Japanese relatives of the dead sailors held special memorial services for their long-lost loved ones, while divers closed and welded shut the hatch.

A tank sits in an odd position on the slightly tilted deck of the *Nippo Maru*, a cargo ship that went down with new artillery pieces, trucks, mines and ammunition.

The stern of the *Nippo* was destroyed by bombs, but the ship is upright on the bottom, listing a bit to one side. The bridge section of the *Nippo Maru* is intact and is an exciting discovery for divers, since the shipwreck was only recently found.

Clark Graham, who went to Truk as a Peace Corps volunteer, stayed on, opening a dive business with his wife Chineina. Clark enjoys showing divers some of the many airplane wrecks in the lagoon. A Betty Bomber, shot down after takeoff, is fairly intact except for the cockpit area. Divers can swim into the fuselage of the twin-engined Japanese bomber, examining the radio gear.

A large Japanese four-engined Emily Flying Boat lies upside down on the bottom,

Clark Graham on Truk.

Clark on his dive boat.

her propellers and engine cowlings dug into the sand. The Emily's instrument panels are still there and divers, rubbing off some of the marine growth, can even read the dials.

Truk Lagoon is protected as an underwater museum. Divers are not permitted to remove any souvenirs or artifacts from the ships. Truk hopes that for as long as these iron relics of the war remain, divers can enjoy swimming among them, discovering the largest navy in the world that never sails.

Diver exploring sunken Japanese flying boat on bottom of lagoon.

7   The Quest for the *Titanic* and *Andrea Doria*

AS a young man, Peter Gimbel was fascinated with diving. He was working at a Wall Street brokerage firm when he heard news on the radio that the majestic Italian passenger liner *Andrea Doria* was struck by another ship in the north Atlantic. At the office he scanned the news ticker machine for word about the ship. When the news flashed that the liner sank, Peter Gimbel decided to dive it. He took time off, flew to Nantucket Island and chartered a fishing boat to take him and his party to the site of the sinking.

His fascination with the legendary liner brought him back again and again, and he finally mounted a major expedition to explore and film the wreck and to recover one of the ship's safes.

We will join Peter Gimbel on this exciting expedition to the *Andrea Doria* and others as they search for the greatest leviathan of all time, the fabled White Star liner *Titanic*.

THE *Andrea Doria*, the ultimate trans-Atlantic luxury liner, sank in the Atlantic about fifty miles south of Nantucket Island on

July 26, 1956. The 700-foot-long liner collided with the Swedish ship *Stockholm* in dense fog.

The *Andrea Doria* sank on her side in 235 feet of water. The depth and ocean currents, coupled with prevailing bad weather except for a couple of months during the summer, makes diving on the shipwreck extremely difficult.

Immediately after the *Andrea Doria* sank, Peter Gimbel, a member of the department store family, hoping to get a scoop for *Life* magazine, dove on the shipwreck and managed to take the first underwater pictures. Thus began a more than twenty-five-year fascination with the wreck of this ship.

Peter Gimbel (in suit and tie) opening safe of Andrea Doria *on live TV.*

The mystery of the *Andrea Doria* had lured many divers to challenge the depths in the hopes of salvaging treasure from the ship. One group of commercial divers dove on the wreck and used explosives to blow off the bronze statue of Admiral Andrea Doria, which is now said to decorate a cocktail lounge somewhere. Other youthful adventurers designed an underwater habitat in 1973 and lowered it over the wreck. This saturation diving system was the first professional attempt to put divers down on the *Doria* in a diving system that would enable them to live underwater.

Once the divers saturate, that is their bodies completely absorb the breathing gases under the great pressure at their working depth, the divers can live at the depth where they are working. They are able to

Banknotes from Andrea Doria *being treated by conservationist.*

The banknotes as they were brought out of the Andrea Doria *safe.*

rest and sleep in a dry chamber and leave it to dive on the shipwreck, and not have to surface after each dive to decompress. Only when the job is finished, are the divers brought to the surface still under "working" pressure in their diving bell or habitat. They are then transferred to a decompression chamber and "brought back" to surface pressure in a comfortable dry environment.

The 1973 project succeeded in cutting a hole in the *Andrea Doria*'s hull in the area of the ship's first-class foyer. Bad weather and difficult conditions plagued the work and finally time and money ran out and the project had to be abandoned.

Silver certificate and Italian mille lire note from Andrea Doria's safe preserved in acrylic.

Salvaged from sunken Italian liner Andrea Doria

Returning to the *Andrea Doria* in 1981, Peter Gimbel and his wife Elga decided to extend the size of the hole cut by the team in 1973. They took with them a team of professional divers and photographers.

A safe from the *Andrea Doria's* first-class bank was found on the ship under debris and silt. Divers attached cables to it to haul it up out of the wreck. Once the Credito Italiano bank safe was brought to the surface, it was placed in sea water in a tank on the dive support ship. Eventually, the safe was transferred to the shark tank of the New York Aquarium in Coney Island, New York. To add drama to their film, the Gimbels decided to open the safe live on television when their feature film was aired.

While the treasure recovered from the wreck of the *Andrea Doria* was minimal, consisting for the most part of dishes and service from the first-class dining room, along with Italian lire banknotes, some United States silver certificates and other paper money, the adventure of divers conquering the depths to explore legendary shipwrecks has inspired imaginations of armchair explorers around the world.

FOR generations, stories of the sinking of the *Titanic* have fired the imaginations of writers, historians and adventurers. It was said to be the finest ship ever built. Unsinkable, it was the ultimate in engineering and technology.

The *Titanic* set sail on her maiden voyage in 1912. The ship rose 175 feet from keel to funnel heads and had an overall length of 882 feet, with fifteen decks. The ship

Ad for film, SOS Titanic, *showing conception of sinking.*

weighed 46,328 tons. Passengers dined in opulence on the White Star liner when she left Southampton, England bound for New York on April 12, 1912. While her 2,224 passengers dined, the liner sped through the North Atlantic at 22.5 knots. The captain ignored warnings that there were icebergs in the area, refusing to reduce speed. When lookouts spotted a berg, it was too late. The *Titanic* struck at 11:40 P.M. The ship was approximately three hundred miles southeast of Cape Race, Newfoundland, when she hit. The iceberg ripped a three-hundred-foot-gash in her iron plates below the water line, flooding five of her sixteen watertight compartments. Engineers had boasted that the *Titanic* was unsinkable, even with four compartments flooded.

The *Titanic* radioed for help, but to no avail. A nearby ship had shut down its radio and thought the distress flares the *Titanic* sent up were fireworks.

At 2:20 A.M. on April 15, 1912, the *Titanic* sank, and with her from 1,503 to 1,517 passengers and crew perished in the frigid waters of the North Atlantic.

The ocean where the *Titanic* sank is twelve thousand feet deep. The ocean floor in that area is laced with canyons. Deep ocean storms, known as benthic storms, created by deep currents flowing in different directions, sometimes churn the ocean bottom into murky muddy water, limiting visibility.

An oil wildcatter from Texas by the name of Jack Grimm, whose exploits included the search for the Loch Ness monster and Noah's ark, embarked on a project with Columbia University's Lamont-Doherty Geological Laboratories to locate the position of the *Titanic,* then to lower deep sea cam-

Hap Perry with unmanned deep sea submersible capable of exploring shipwrecks in the very deep ocean reaches.

eras over the site on cables to try to film the wreckage.

Sophisticated sonar was developed that would scan the ocean floor and print the profile or outline of what the sonar recorded on a chart aboard their research ship. But, if the *Titanic* had fallen into one of the huge ocean craters or canyons on the bottom, the scientists would have no chance at all of finding the ship with sonar.

The pictures recorded on the charts in the vicinity of where the *Titanic* was reported sunk encouraged the scientists. While bad weather forced them to abandon the project early, they felt that they had located, at last, the ship that had resulted in the most infamous maritime tragedy in modern history.

Professor Bill Ryan with Titanic *computer printout.*

Bill Ryan with deep sea camera used to film Titanic.

Using the information gleaned from the first *Titanic* expedition as a base, a joint French-American team of scientists recently lowered a camera-carrying robot to the ocean bottom. Scientists aboard the research vessel were elated when the pictures beamed back showed the legendary liner on the ocean floor almost two-and-a-half miles below.

The cameras showed the *Titanic* to be almost upright on the bottom. Passengers' luggage, bottles of wine and various items from the *Titanic* were scattered on the bottom near the shipwreck.

When the *Titanic* went down, a jewel-encrusted edition of the *Rubaiyat,* some 200 million dollars' worth of jewels from Antwerp and a countless fortune in personal property of the passengers was lost with the ship. There are high hopes of using a submarine equipped with robots to enter the *Titanic* and recover some of the treasure. The extreme depth and difficult ocean conditions will require careful preparation if the *Titanic* is ever to yield up her treasure from the deep.

8   Hidden Wrecks in Harbors Near Home

FOR the average person, sometimes the exotic and faraway is beyond reach and can only be enjoyed by reading about the exploits of others. Yet almost every place where people have built settlements near the sea, interesting things can be found among discards and trash they abandoned, heaved over or lost at the water's edge. Lakes, rivers, even harbors near home can provide a gold mine of discovery for the curious, willing to devote a little time to research.

THE owner of the small marina came out of a hut he used as an office. He was trying to persuade the Corps of Engineers' supervisor to leave intact a section of the shoreline so that boats could still be kept there. While that wasn't possible, the archaeologists for the corps found out some interesting facts from the old-timer about shipwrecks thrown up in the mud nearby.

"They used to sneak in here at night and leave the old ships to rot," Captain Harry Rydquist said aboard the Corps of Engineers Harbor Patrol Boat *Hudson*. "We'd try and catch them, but couldn't." He smiled, remembering the thirty-five years he'd worked around New York Harbor.

Dig at Water Street where the land has been filled over old shipwrecks abandoned in early days of Dutch settlement.

Dig at Water Street, South Street Seaport.

Bows of old wooden ship abandoned in New York Harbor.

The old hulks both men were referring to were wooden ships, canal barges, dry docks and assorted derelicts that had outlived their usefulness and were abandoned in the mud flats around New York Harbor. The ships had been left to time and the crabs and few, if any, remembered how or when the old derelicts got there or what the ships were.

The state of New Jersey decided to take advantage of a federal government grant to clean up the harbor area in back of the Statue of Liberty to create a park. Scores of old wooden ships and barges littered the muddy creeks and marshlands. The Corps of Engineers had the responsibility of keeping the harbor free of floating debris that was a hazard to navigation. With every tide and storm, wood from the derelict ships would break free and float into the harbor.

Before the Corps of Engineers can authorize a project, an environmental and archaeological survey must be made to be sure important things won't be destroyed. It was during the survey around New York that marine archaeologists discovered that many of these old ships were unique examples of American shipbuilding. Some were the last remaining examples of certain types of steamers and schooners.

Peter Throckmorton, one of the marine archaeologists hired to work on the harbor shipwreck project, had only recently returned from Greece where he and George Bass had found and excavated sunken ships

Peter Throckmorton (white beard) with Corps of Engineers' expert at site of watermelon barges in New York Harbor.

from the golden age of Hellenic civilization. Tramping through the mud, Pete and Dr. Ira Abrams poked around the old ships in New York Harbor, just as excited at some of their finds.

Some of the ships were found to have been converted for special use around the harbor. Pete and Ira found two hulks they called watermelon barges because of their unusual shapes. Old steam tugs and harbor lighters, barges from the days of the Erie canal and assorted wooden sailing vessels dotted the abandoned corners of the harbor.

Some pieces of the wrecks were saved and displayed in the Brooklyn headquarters of the National Maritime Historical Society. Some of the wrecks themselves were broken up by the contractors, carted out to sea in barges and burned.

After a couple of hours on the first day, the archaeologists had gathered up a bushel basket full of deadeyes. These deadeyes are round hardwood blocks with holes in them, which were used to make the rigging fast on sailing ships. The wood was usually lignum vitae, the hardest wood of all, so dense that it will not float. Today, deadeyes have been replaced by stainless steel turnbuckles. Deadeyes are an interesting collector's item left over from the days of sail power.

Captain Rydquist and Corps of Engineers Inspector Joe Monagas still patrol areas around the harbor where derelict ships remain to be discovered. Pointing to Shooter's Island, in the middle of the channel between New Jersey and Staten Island, the men indicated the final resting place of many old wooden ships.

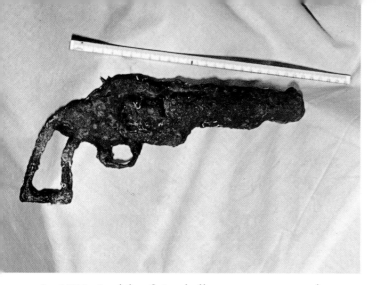

An 1876 pistol found in shallow water, apparently thrown in from New York's waterfront.

ANYONE with an interest in maritime history can organize an excursion around the harbors and ports near home. Discovering old shipwrecks, taking pictures, and then doing the detective work to identify them can be an interesting club, school, scout or church project. Rivers and canals far inland have yielded interesting paddle-wheelers and steamboats, some dating from the Civil War.

Lakes too have their share of shipwrecks, abandoned in coves, so close to shore and obvious that they are often overlooked by amateur historians.

Admirers of artifacts at the film festival and show in New York where divers proudly display their souvenirs recovered from the deep.

Harbor archaeology can be an interesting way to discover valuable historic artifacts not far from home. Perhaps some day, lucky searchers will find Captain Kidd's treasure.

In 1951, a fisherman hunting turtles in a place called Ship Bottom, New Jersey, found a bronze plaque marked "William Kidd, Master, *Quedagh*." Still missing though, is the treasure cache of this famous privateer captain. Until he was hung on London's execution dock in 1701, Captain Kidd was a British privateer. Although he

Author John Christopher Fine (gray) with Mark Obermeier prepare to dive on the wreck of a German submarine sunk off Block Island, New York. This was the last casualty of WW II, lost when depth charged by American destroyers after the war was actually declared over.

owned property on Pearl Street in lower Manhattan, Captain Kidd set out to pillage French and Spanish ships.

In 1698, Captain Kidd and his men captured the *Quedagh Merchant,* a Moorish ship. After his crew deserted to another pirate, Captain Kidd was left with a handful of loyal sailors, a share of the booty and the captured merchant ship *Quedagh*. He returned to New York, and, it is said, he hid his loot in various places around New York and Connecticut.

Captain Kidd was finally hung at Tilbury, England, and his body, tarred and wrapped in iron hoops, was suspended over the water so every boat passing would see his body. Rather than discouraging piracy, Captain Kidd's bones hanging in the breeze may have encouraged pirates not to get caught. In any event, most of Captain Kidd's treasure has yet to be found, perhaps buried somewhere around the port and harbors of New York, Gardiner's Island and all along the eastern seaboard.

Perhaps a lucky beachcomber poking around the harbors or back bays will someday stumble upon a treasure chest and find the lost pirate treasure of Captain Kidd or some other freebooter who plied his trade in the heyday of piracy.

9 Museums of Old Ships

A FAMILY holiday can be turned into an adventure by exploring museums devoted to maritime displays. The heritage of all major civilizations is connected with the sea, and seafaring nations often exhibit that heritage with pride. Learning from history can be as exciting as it is rewarding. Visiting museums of old ships is one way of learning about history. Often a person can participate in history by joining any of the many volunteer projects offered by maritime museums and ship preservation projects.

ANYONE with an interest in shipwrecks should begin by visiting museums or ship restorations. There are many seaports that feature examples of old windships and steamers, some offer tours, classes, seminars and films about shipbuilding and ship history.

One of the best known seaport restorations is in the old Fulton Fish Market area of Manhattan. New York's South Street Seaport occupies restored buildings along the waterfront and maintains piers where re-

Op-sail in South Street Seaport, New York.

South Street Seaport gala celebration.

stored ships are on display. The museum owns a Gloucester fishing boat, the Ambrose lightship, steam tugs and a ferry.

Programs developed by the seaport include the extensive restoration of two large iron-hulled square-rigged vessels, the *Peking* and the *Wavertree*. Visitors can go aboard the South Street vessels and talk to museum workmen and curators who are in the process of restoring the ships.

The museum library and galleries have books, drawings and research materials about ships and shipwrecks, maritime history and marine archaeology. An artifact recovered from a shipwreck by divers can be brought to experts at the South Street Museum and sometimes identified, leading to discovery of the name of the wreck, or at least dating the find.

The South Street Seaport plays host to festivals of the sea. Their docks are often a port of call for sailing vessels and training ships for navies and maritime academies around the world.

The National Maritime Historical Society located in San Francisco, is a wonderful source of information. The N.M.H.S. is staffed by volunteers dedicated to old ships and maritime history. Taking time to visit the museums and talking with staff people can often provide excellent contacts and ideas for projects to locate and identify shipwrecks.

At Mystic Seaport in Connecticut, a restoration of the whaling ship *Henry Morgan* is on display along with marine artifacts from the days when Yankee whalers set out from Mystic for long voyages around the world. Frequently, when a wooden shipwreck is discovered, all that remains is that portion of the hull that was buried in the sand or mud, protected from boring teredo worms that eat away wood underwater. Ocean currents and storms also break up and destroy wooden wrecks underwater. Sometimes only pieces of a wreck can be found. Knowing something about how a wooden ship is made will help divers identify a shipwreck. Very few old wrecks are discovered with their nameplates intact on the stern.

Old brigs like the ninety-seven-foot-long *Carthaginian* are other wharfside attractions.

The *Carthaginian*, built in 1920 in Kiel, Germany, at the Krupp shipworks, was a two-masted schooner used as a cement carrier in the Baltic Sea. The *Carthaginian* is now on display in the port of Lahaina on the island of Maui in Hawaii. Another square-rigger, the *Falls of Clyde,* is also on display in Hawaii, in the port district of Honolulu.

Shipwrecks have been used as memorials to war and to major naval battles. At Pearl Harbor, the sunken wreckage of the battleship *Arizona* is a national memorial to the crewmen who lost their lives during the Japanese attack. Pearl Harbor also features the *Bowfin* or SS 287, a United States World War II submarine.

Visiting the *Bowfin* memorial is an excel-

The Carthaginian *in Lahaina.*

View of Pearl Harbor Memorial built over the wreckage of U.S. Battleship Arizona.

Turret of the Arizona.

Bowfin *at Pearl Harbor (far right).*

lent way for shipwreck divers to get an idea of the configuration of a World War II submarine. Built in 1941, the 311-foot-long sub saw action in Pacific waters off Mindanao, the South China Sea, the Sulu Sea off Borneo, Palau, and off the coast of Japan. The *Bowfin* sank a total of thirty-eight enemy ships amounting to 109,230 tons.

After visiting the *Bowfin,* divers once were able to enjoy a dive over the U.S.S. *Bluegill,*

a submarine deliberately scuttled by the United States Navy off the island of Maui for use as a diver-training area. After some sport divers were stricken with the bends surfacing from a dive to the *Bluegill,* the Navy lifted the submarine from the ocean floor and dropped it in extremely deep water beyond the range of sport divers.

Models of underwater shipwreck excavation sites are set up in Washington at the Smithsonian Institution Museum of History and Technology. On display also are examples of diving and salvage equipment as well as treasure and artifacts recovered from sunken ships. The gondola *Philadelphia,* recovered from Lake Champlain is also on display. The *Philadelphia* was one of the boats used against the British by Benedict Arnold during the Revolutionary War.

Gondola Philadelphia *in Smithsonian.*

Diver exploring the submarine Bluegill *in deep water off Lahaina, Maui, Hawaii, before the navy moved it to much deeper water to keep sport divers off it.*

MANY shipwrecks are found in areas where captains and crews were forced to abandon their perilous voyages. Near Cape Horn at the tip of South America in the South Atlantic off the Falkland (Malvinas) Islands, many old square-rigged ships and Yankee clippers lie abandoned, victims of storms and arduous crossings, battering seas and bad weather.

Some states are deliberately sinking old ships in shallow water offshore to provide

Shot of shipwreck on Isles of Scilly from Frank Gibson collection; his family chronicled sinkings from the very early days.

Diver explores sunken wreck off Miami. These wrecks have been sunk as part of a reef building project and have proved quite successful.

habitats for marine organisms. Scientists have found that in a relatively short time these shipwrecks form artificial reefs, attracting fish and marine growth, and also providing interesting diving for week-end scuba enthusiasts.

Learning about shipwrecks and the sea can be a rewarding experience. After doing the research, donning a mask and flippers and hunting up treasures and artifacts becomes a fascinating hobby. Amateur shipwreck hunters can also join with local museums in volunteer projects and work on ship restoration projects.

Prow of a sunken ship off Miami.

I TOLD a friend's mother about a Florida beach where, after every storm, coins wash up from Spanish galleons sunk off shore. The mother, father and son took a trip with friends to Fort Pierce and searched the beach with metal detectors. Sure enough, in a clump of rock and coral that gave a detector reading, they discovered a valuable minted piece of eight dated 1714. There is treasure near home and with a little research and some simple tools, you can be well on your way to finding it, just as my Florida friends did.

Charles Garrett has probably designed more treasure detectors than anyone. From his electronics firm in Texas, Garrett's metal detectors are shipped all over the world and have been responsible for making a lot of amateur and professional treasure hunters rich.

Garrett himself is an avid scuba diver who has designed underwater metal detectors that can be tuned to detect gold and silver objects buried under coral or sand and ignore tin cans and worthless bits of iron.

A diver can even tune in the detector to

avoid outside interference from mineral salts in the water and other unwanted signals. By passing the search coil of a detector over the ocean bottom, a diver can cover a large area in a relatively short time.

Doing a little research first can help amateur treasure hunters locate the best spots to snorkel or dive for treasure. Very often, valuable finds can be made just a short distance from a diver's home. Areas near shore often offer the amateur treasure hunter the best likelihood of success.

Using a metal detector near docks used by water skiers often yields an assortment of gold chains, rings, earrings and medals, which fell off when the unlucky skier took a

Author (with Garrett metal detector) and Jack Pennel exploring Florida beach near where galleon sank offshore.

One of Mel Fisher's divers using a metal detector underwater.

tumble. Care must always be used when snorkeling near a dock, and precautions must be taken to avoid boat traffic and broken glass or sharp objects on the bottom.

In upstate New York, divers traced the history of an area around a lake from early Colonial times until the turn of the century. The local librarian and the town's historical society were quite helpful in providing books and original maps. An island in the middle of the lake was the last meeting place for a branch of the Iroquois Indians. The early maps and photographs pictured luxury hotels that catered to a rich summer tourist trade. There was even a paddlewheel ferry

Author with class on Lake Mahopac where many antiques were found, including coins, antique handblown bottles and china.

boat that took visitors on a cruise around the lake.

A snorkeler or diver will have the best chances searching areas where people congregated, where they would have been most likely to lose, drop or throw things into the water. Using the old maps as a reference point, hotel sites were chosen as the best place to start looking for treasure. The old hotels were no longer standing, in some cases demolished or destroyed by fire. Yet their foundations were easily found and remnants of piers the guests used for fishing and boating were still marked by piles of stones and debris.

Organizing a search in water near shore not even a foot deep, the divers almost immediately began digging up antique bottles and china dishes. Many of the old bottles were hand blown in oblong torpedo shapes, with marks that indicated they had been made in England and Ireland. Early English china pitchers and bowls were found, along with an assortment of swords, knives, tools and a few coins dated as early as 1803.

Of course, the divers also recovered a lot of modern lost items, including fishing tackle, an inexpensive watch, and invariably, old refrigerators, toilet bowls and assorted junk. In all, the adventurous divers enjoyed a day's outing, had a good time and friendly cookout on shore while finding some fairly nice artifacts — discovered with only a little research, not far from home.

DIVERS who take time to ask residents about local shipwrecks, sites where early ferry boats landed, where Indian campgrounds or early settlements were located are often rewarded for their efforts by finding historical artifacts.

On Lake George, New York, an area of early American Colonial settlement and activity during the Revolutionary War, divers often find clay smoking pipes, old bottles,

An 1803 penny found by author in one foot of water while snorkeling in Lake Mahopac.

tools and Indian artifacts. Not far away, on Lake Champlain, one of the original boats used by Benedict Arnold to repel the British was recovered almost intact. As mentioned earlier, the ship was salvaged and is now on exhibit in the Smithsonian Museum.

SOME history buffs will remember the story about His Majesty O'Keefe, the legendary figure who was shipwrecked on the island of Yap. Nursed back to health and befriended by the local people, David Dean O'Keefe saw his chance to make a fortune in the copra trade if only he could get the local people to cooperate. No one had yet succeeded in motivating the islanders to work at all, let alone gather and dry coconuts for copra.

The Yapese valued stone money, which

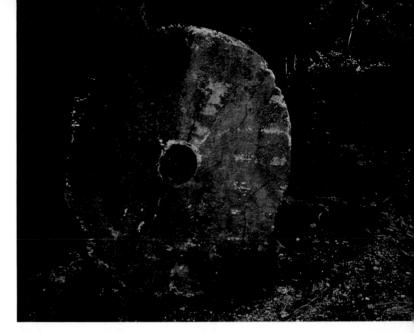

Stone money of Yap.

they would quarry on the island of Palau, crossing the open ocean in their fragile canoes, bringing the stones back to Yap only at great peril to their own lives. When O'Keefe was well enough, he caught a ship

back to Hong Kong, formed a partnership with a merchant who bankrolled him and sailed back to Yap in his own trading ship. With the big sailing vessel O'Keefe took the Yapese to Palau where they loaded up on stone money, promoted O'Keefe to a kind of king and in return collected copra for him. O'Keefe made his fortune on Yap, living on an island offshore.

Snorkeling in the shallow water around the ruins of O'Keefe's mansion, a diver can find many artifacts used by His Majesty O'Keefe. Bottles, china, jugs, plates and assorted remnants of the O'Keefe era abound in the water not one foot deep.

Author on His Majesty O'Keefe's Island on Yap, with finds discovered in shallow water, proving that David Dean O'Keefe really lived like a king.

THE key element in any search for historical artifacts is to search where old-time residents would have been likely to lose or throw away items that now may have great historical value.

Many weekend divers are lured by the adventure of diving on shipwrecks sunk off the Atlantic seaboard. There are hundreds of ships in the relatively shallow water of the continental shelf, off New York and New Jersey. During World War II, German submarines would wait just offshore to torpedo American and Allied shipping.

A veteran wreck diver, Charlie Stratton, has become something of a legend on the East Coast. Charlie has been discovering old

Veteran shipwreck diver Charlie Stratton aboard his ship the Bottom Time *off New Jersey's coast.*

shipwrecks for more than twenty-five years. He carefully guards the location of his favorite wrecks, taking only a few friends, whom he can trust, out to dive them.

Charlie uses a military surplus echolocation device that enables him to find wrecks underwater. The sonar was used during wartime to locate enemy submarines. The device sends sound waves out and records them on a chart when they bounce back off an object underwater. When a possible wreck is located, Charlie runs over the site with a recording fathometer. The fathometer measures depth and records the profile of the bottom on a paper chart.

Divers enjoy recovering portholes, and brass and copper spikes and fittings from old shipwrecks. One sometimes comes aboard Charlie's boat with the ultimate of prizes, a ship's bell, brass telegraph or spoked helm.

Most of the wrecks on the East Coast are in shallow water about eighty feet deep, since the continental shelf extends a long distance offshore. Wreck diving is exciting. For trained divers going out with experienced guides like Charlie Stratton, diving over old ships can be a great adventure in relatively shallow water not far from home.

THE SEA conceals many treasures. Shipwrecks are history lost beneath the waves. While adventurers search the depths to find and explore sunken galleons, weekend divers enjoy shipwreck diving as a popular sport.

The romance and adventure that have challenged seafaring men for generations have been placed within reach of modern scientists and explorers willing to don mask, fins and snorkel to explore the ocean realm.

The oceans are a vast continent of unexplored inner space. Sunken ships offer a challenge, hold out an adventure, provide keys that may unlock hidden secrets of history, secrets concealed with cargoes lost to time.

A diver works an air lift back and forth between the crevices in the rocks to expose coins and valuable artifacts, Isles of Scilly, United Kingdom.

Bibliography

LISTING BOOKS in a bibliography can be helpful in providing other reference sources which may treat specific topics in greater detail. More important than a bibliography for a person doing serious shipwreck research is to become familiar with their local library. A reference librarian will always take time to help by describing how reference books on treasure, shipwrecks, maritime history, pirates, salvage and nautical archaeology are arranged and how other source materials can be located in the card catalog.

Interlibrary loans can be arranged if materials needed for research are not available on local library shelves. Librarians will be able to help researchers with local history, and can often provide the names and telephone numbers of local historians or knowledgeable people in the community.

The local library is of great importance to those who seek information about lakes, rivers, harbors and early settlements. Libraries maintain microfilm copies of old newspapers which will have carried stories of sinkings and shipwrecks, describing the cargo and salvage attempts.

The National Archives in Washington, D.C. has a large collection of U.S. Naval photographs, films and documents. The South Street Seaport Museum Library and the Atlantic Mutual Insurance Company Library, both located in Manhattan, near the Lower East Side waterfront in New York City have large collections of books and documents about ships and ship sinkings. The Mariner's Museum in Newport News, Virginia, also has a very large collection of old ship photographs and archive materials. All of these libraries maintain complete sets of the Lloyd's Register of Ships and the American Bureau of Shipping Record along with other important reference collections.

Some books of interest that provide good reading and a starting point for research source material, include:

Bass, George, *A History of Seafaring Based on Underwater Archaeology*, London, Thames & Hudson, New York, Walker & Co., 1972

Burgess, Robert F., *Sinkings, Salvages and Shipwrecks*, New York, American Heritage Press, 1970

Garrett, Charles, F., *Successful Coin Hunting*, Dallas, Texas, Ram Publishing Co., 1981

Gianfrotta, Piero and Pomey, Patrice, *l'Archeologie Sous La Mer* (in French), Paris, Fernand Nathan, 1980

Hoffman, William and Grimm, Jack, *Beyond Reach, The Search for the Titanic*, New York, Beaufort Books, 1982

Lyttle, Richard B., *Waves Across the Past*, New York, Atheneum, 1981

Marx, Robert F., *The Lure of Sunken Treasure*, New York, David McKay Co., 1973

Marx, Robert F., *The Underwater Dig*, New York, Henry Walck, 1975

Metery, Michel, *Tamaya* (The history of the sinking of ships in St. Pierre Bay, Martinique, written in French) Grenoble, France, Glenat, 1984

National Geographic Society, *Undersea Treasures*, Washington, National Geographic Society, 1974

Norris, Martin J., *The Law of Salvage*, Vol. 3A in multi-volume set of Benedict on Admiralty (Available in any county or federal courthouse library or university law school library), New York, Matthew Bender, 1983

Olesky, Walter, *Treasures of the Deep*, New York, Messner, 1984

Throckmorton, Peter, *Diving For Treasure*, New York, Viking Press, 1977

Tompkins, B.A., *Treasure*, New York, N.Y. Times Books, 1979

Index